CHICAGO

MARC TYLER NOBLEMAN

WORLD ALMANAC® LIBRARY

Please visit our web site at: www.worldalmanaclibrary.com
For a free color catalog describing World Almanac® Library's list of high-quality books
and multimedia programs, call 1-800-848-2928 (USA) or 1-800-387-3178 (Canada).
World Almanac® Library's fax: (414) 332-3567.

Library of Congress Cataloging-in-Publication Data

Nobleman, Marc Tyler.
    Chicago / by Marc Tyler Nobleman.
        p. cm. — (Great cities of the world)
    Includes bibliographical references and index.
    ISBN 0-8368-5036-X (lib. bdg.)
    ISBN 0-8368-5196-X (softcover)
    1. Chicago (Ill.)—Juvenile literature. I. Title. II. Series.
F548.33.N63   2004
977.3'11—dc22   2004045525

First published in 2005 by
World Almanac® Library
330 West Olive Street, Suite 100
Milwaukee, WI 53212 USA

Copyright © 2005 by World Almanac® Library.

Produced by Discovery Books
Editor: Helen Dwyer
Series designers: Laurie Shock, Keith Williams
Designer and page production: Ian Winton
Photo researcher: Rachel Tisdale
Maps and diagrams: Stefan Chabluk
Maps: Stefan Chabluk
World Almanac® Library editorial direction: Mark J. Sachner
World Almanac® Library editor: Gini Holland
World Almanac® Library art direction: Tammy West
World Almanac® Library graphic design: Scott M. Krall
World Almanac® Library production: Jessica Morris

Photo credits: Art Directors & Trip/Ask Images: p. 32; Art Directors & Trip/Viesti Collection: pp. 7, 30; Corbis: pp. 11, 23;
Corbis/Bettmann: p. 15; Corbis/Daniel Lainé: p. 21; Corbis/Duomo: p. 36; Corbis/Joseph Sohm/ChromoSohm Inc.: p. 38;
Corbis/Joseph Sohm/Visions of America: p. 27; Corbis/Owaki-Kulla: p. 4; Corbis/Ralf-Finn Hestoft: pp. 12, 25, 29, 43;
Corbis/Reuters: pp. 26, 33; Corbis/Richard Cummins: pp. 16, 19, 20; Corbis/Robert Holmes: p. 41; Corbis/Robert Maass:
p. 35; Corbis/Sandy Felsenthal: pp. 22, 42; Eye Ubiquitous/D. Forman: p. 37; Gareth Stevens/M. Sachner: p. 24; James Davis
Worldwide: p. 40; North Wind Picture Archives: pp. 8, 9

**Cover caption: The Sears Tower rules the evening skyline in downtown Chicago (photograph reproduced by permission
of Corbis/Richard Cummins).**

Printed in the United States of America

1 2 3 4 5 6 7 8 9 08 07 06 05 04

Contents

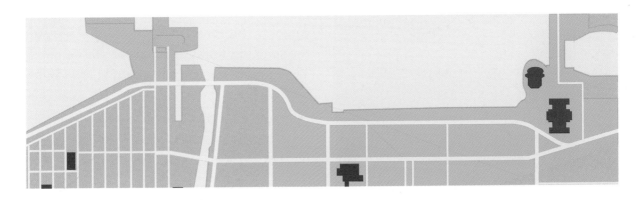

Introduction

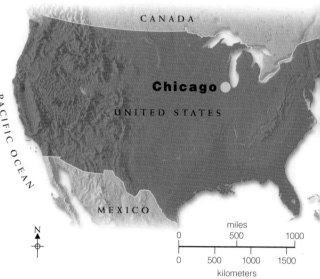

In less than two hundred years, thousands of people, many of them born outside the United States, have worked together to turned a region of lakeside marshland into one of the greatest cities on Earth. The city of Chicago is now the cultural, industrial, and financial center of the nation's midsection and the center of the U.S. transportation system.

Center of the Midwest

Chicago is the United States' third most populous city, after New York and Los Angeles. Although it is the largest city in the state of Illinois, it is not the state capital. That title belongs to Springfield, 185 miles

◄ *The city of Chicago is known for its contrasting views, both urban and natural, which take on a new beauty after the sun has set.*

(298 kilometers) southwest. Nonetheless, much attention in the state—and in some ways, the nation—is focused on Chicago.

City of Extremes

Standing tall on a plain at the southwestern tip of Lake Michigan (a vast freshwater lake), temperatures regularly dip below freezing in winter and stay there. When winter cold couples with the wind that blows off Lake Michigan, most Chicagoans spend as little time as necessary outside.

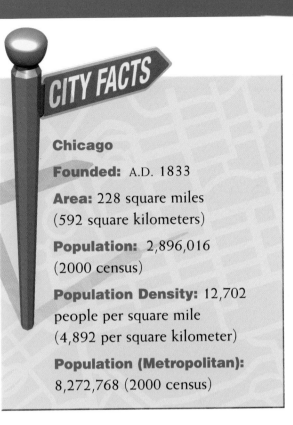

CITY FACTS

Chicago

Founded: A.D. 1833

Area: 228 square miles (592 square kilometers)

Population: 2,896,016 (2000 census)

Population Density: 12,702 people per square mile (4,892 per square kilometer)

Population (Metropolitan): 8,272,768 (2000 census)

Windy City

Upon hearing Chicago's nickname "the Windy City," many assume this refers to weather, but people have debated other possible origins and meanings. One theory claims that New York newspaper editor Charles Dana coined the phrase in 1893. Dana felt that Chicago politicians bragged too much about the good qualities of their city and described them as "windy," meaning long-winded or overly talkative. Years before Dana's remark, however, in the mid-1880s, at least two other newspapers used the term "windy city." They were not commenting on the bone-chilling winter winds commonly associated with Chicago. Instead, they were expressing thanks for the refreshing breezes that blew into the city from Lake Michigan on muggy summer days. Today, the city is often windy for a different reason. Chicago's many tall buildings create canyons that frequently channel winds blowing in from Lake Michigan.

The average temperature in January is 25° Fahrenheit (–4 ° Celsius). Most winters bring heavy snowfall. The average temperature in July is a comfortable 75°F (24°C), although higher temperatures and humidity from the lake often cause people to turn on their air conditioners during the summer.

"It is hopeless for the occasional visitor to try to keep up with Chicago—she outgrows his prophecies faster than he can make them. She is always a novelty; for she is never the Chicago you saw when you passed through the last time."

—Mark Twain, writer, *Life on the Mississippi*, 1883.

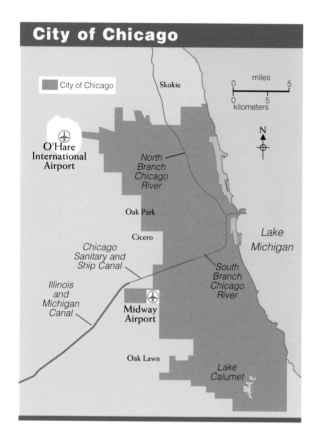

City of Chicago

City of Chicago
Skokie
miles 0 5
kilometers 0 5
N
O'Hare International Airport
North Branch Chicago River
Oak Park
Cicero
Lake Michigan
Chicago Sanitary and Ship Canal
South Branch Chicago River
Illinois and Michigan Canal
Midway Airport
Oak Lawn
Lake Calumet

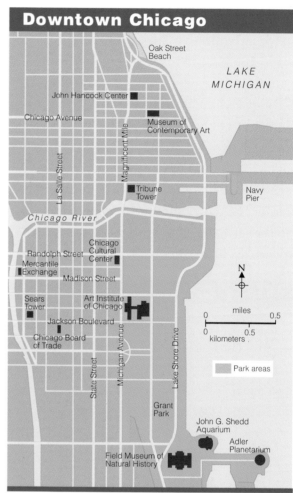

Downtown Chicago

Oak Street Beach
John Hancock Center
Chicago Avenue
LAKE MICHIGAN
Museum of Contemporary Art
La Salle Street
Magnificent Mile
Tribune Tower
Navy Pier
Chicago River
Chicago Cultural Center
Randolph Street
Mercantile Exchange
Madison Street
Sears Tower
Art Institute of Chicago
Jackson Boulevard
Chicago Board of Trade
State Street
Michigan Avenue
Lake Shore Drive
miles 0 0.5
kilometers 0 0.5
N
Park areas
Grant Park
John G. Shedd Aquarium
Adler Planetarium
Field Museum of Natural History

Lake Michigan

Lake Michigan is the third largest of the five Great Lakes and the world's sixth largest freshwater lake. Hugging the lake shore, Chicago has been a major port city since its founding. The port, which links the Great Lakes and an inland river system that feeds the Mississippi, is at the intersection of many railroads and highways. Ships and barges can reach both the Atlantic Ocean and the Gulf of Mexico from Chicago. Its lakeside location is ideal for shipbuilding, an industry that began in Chicago in 1835. The lake brings prosperity as a trade route and provides drinking water for the city. Chicagoans also relax on the lakeshore, swim and fish in its waters, enjoy harbor tours, and sail boats on it.

City Layout

Chicago is an easy city to navigate because its streets are organized in a grid—centered on the intersection of Madison Street and State Street—and the whole of its eastern side is bordered by Lake Michigan. From the lake, the Chicago River winds through the core of the city, then divides into two branches.

Chicago's downtown Loop is bounded by the two branches of the Chicago River and by Lake Michigan. The Loop got its name from the elevated tracks of the "El" trains that run in a loop above the center of the district. Chicago's tallest skyscrapers, the financial center, world-class museums, and the Chicago Public Library are all located downtown. During the day, the Loop is crowded with people, but at night it can appear deserted.

Neighborhoods

Radiating out on three sides from the Loop, Chicago is divided into North, West, and South Sides. The North Side is located north and east of the Chicago River. Much of it is affluent, with fashionable neighborhoods, boutiques, and restaurants. A mix of nationalities live on the West Side, situated west of the Chicago River, and the West Side still attracts immigrants today. Most of Chicago's African American population lives on the South Side that borders the southern end of the Loop.

Chicago is located in Cook County, which, along with five adjacent counties, forms the Chicago metropolitan area, popularly known as Chicagoland.

"I adore Chicago. It is the pulse of America."

—Sarah Bernhardt (1844–1923), French actress.

▼ Oak Street Beach is one of several Chicago lakefront recreation areas that are only minutes from downtown.

CHAPTER 1

History of Chicago

People lived on the land that is now Chicago at least ten thousand years ago. By the 1600s, many Native American tribes inhabited the region. Historians are uncertain about which tribe named the area "Chicago" and what the name meant. Some believe it comes from a Native word for "wild onion" or "skunk cabbage," perhaps because the rotting marsh plants in the area at the time had a foul odor. Others think the word is translated as "strong" or "great."

First European Explorers

The first recorded Europeans to pass through the Chicago region were French-Canadian explorer Louis Jolliet and missionary Jacques Marquette. In 1673, Native Americans showed the two men useful land and water routes in the region. These routes were used by fur trappers and traders throughout the 1700s. In 1779, Jean Baptiste Point du Sable, a fur trapper and trader born to a French father and a Haitian mother, established the first permanent non–Native settlement in the Chicago region, near the mouth of the Chicago River.

The United States and a coalition of

◀ In 1673, Louis Jolliet and Jacques Marquette explored the waters of the region that is now Chicago in birchbark canoes. This sculpture on a bridge over the Chicago River commemorates their journey.

1795, which granted the Chicago region to the United States so that the U.S. government could set up a military post on the south bank of the Chicago River. Fort Dearborn was built there in 1803.

New State, New City

Illinois became a state in 1818, and in 1830, before it became a town, Chicago's streets were planned. In 1833, with a population of 350, Chicago incorporated as a town. In 1837, the state of Illinois granted Chicago, now with a population of more than 4,000, a city charter. Yet a period of even greater growth was about to sweep Chicago.

▼ *Fort Dearborn, located where downtown Chicago is today, was the site of a massacre during the War of 1812. Native Americans, allied with the British, killed more than eighty soldiers there.*

"Indian corn, with some smoked meat, constituted all our provisions; with these we embarked—Mr. Jolliet and myself, with five men—in two bark canoes, fully resolved to do and suffer everything for so glorious an undertaking."

—Jacques Marquette, missionary, on exploration of regions including Chicago, 1673.

The Erie Canal, completing a water route between New York City and the Great Lakes, had opened in 1825. The Illinois and Michigan Canal, linking the Great Lakes and the Mississippi River, opened in 1848. These two waterways helped people ship livestock, lumber, and grain through the country. Such economic possibilities

enticed more easterners to head west and lured others from overseas who were eager for work. In the mid-nineteenth century, Irish and German immigrants were among the first to fill industrial jobs in Chicago.

Newcomers found Chicago's lakeside location desirable. Many stayed and started businesses. One such business was Sears, Roebuck and Company, which is still in operation today. Sears was an early leader in the mailorder business. Customers browsed a sales catalog that Sears produced and placed their orders through the mail.

By 1860, the city's population reached 300,000. Within twenty years, it swelled to 500,000, and that figure doubled, exceeding one million, within the next decade, to make Chicago the country's major Midwest city.

Canals, once the main mode of cross-country transportation, were soon eclipsed by railroads. By the mid-1850s, Chicago was the country's center for freight and passenger trains. More railroads were being built, including commuter lines from the suburbs, and more immigrants came to Chicago to help build them.

Industry Booms

By the 1860s, a number of slaughterhouses and meatpackers were scattered around Chicago. To work more efficiently, they purchased land together in Chicago's southwest district. On Christmas Day, 1865, the group opened the Union Stock Yards to process meat for consumption.

"There would be meat that had tumbled out on the floor, in the dirt and sawdust, where the workers had tramped and spit uncounted billions of consumption [tuberculosis] germs. There would be meat stored in great piles in rooms; and the water from leaky roofs would drip over it, and thousands of rats would race about on it."

—Upton Sinclair's description of a Chicago meatpacking factory in his novel *The Jungle*, 1906.

The invention of ice-cooled storage units and refrigerated railroad cars decreased the chance of spoilage during shipping. They also allowed meatpackers to work year-round, not just in cold weather. As a result, the Union Stock Yards became even more successful, and by 1900 they produced 82 percent of the meat sold in the United States.

However, the conditions were abominable for the thousands of immigrants employed in Chicago's meatpacking industry. They labored twelve hours a day in stinking, hot factories where the floors were slippery with animal blood. Even children had jobs there. Upton Sinclair's 1906 book *The Jungle* helped expose the horrible realities of the plants and led to reforms.

A Massive Fire

On the night of October 8, 1871, a fire started on Chicago's West Side, probably in

▲ *After the Great Fire of 1871, the people of Chicago began rebuilding their city almost immediately. Once the ruins cooled enough, they began sweeping rubble into Lake Michigan.*

a barn. The weather was dry and, because most structures were made of wood, the flames raged through much of the city within hours.

Rain began to fall around midnight on October 9. By morning the inferno was out, but the disaster had killed three hundred people, left at least ninety thousand homeless, and incinerated eighteen thousand buildings. Chicagoans were battered but not beaten. Recovery began immediately and moved fast.

"All gone but WIFE, CHILDREN, and ENERGY"

—William Kerfoot, real estate businessman, on a sign put up the day after the fire ended, 1871.

Birth of a Modern City

Out of tragedy came innovation. Chicago was rebuilt more sturdily, in stone and metal. The nine-story Home Insurance Building, considered the world's first steel-framed skyscraper, went up in Chicago in 1885. Many more were built within a short period, along with other handsome pieces of architecture. The city's first elevated train tracks were installed in the 1890s.

The reconstruction of Chicago did not proceed without tension. In 1886, blue-collar workers went on strike because they

University of Chicago

The campus of the University of Chicago (below) sits eight miles south of the Loop. Opened in 1892, the school is one of the world's finest research institutions. More than seventy people associated with the university have won a Nobel Prize. Among its many noteworthy alumni are writer Kurt Vonnegut; astronomer Carl Sagan; John Ashcroft, United States Attorney General under President George W. Bush; and Carol Moseley-Braun, the first female African American United States Senator.

*"Gigantic, willful, young,
Chicago sitteth at the northwest gates."*

—William Vaughn Moody, poet and playwright,
1901.

wanted to limit their workday to eight hours. They also held a demonstration on the West Side. When police tried to break up the gathering, a bomb exploded, and chaos followed. Seven officers and an unknown number of workers died in this tragedy, which was later known as the Haymarket Riot. Another strike, in 1894, against the Pullman railroad car company, was significant because it was one of the earliest instances in the United States of white and black workers uniting to demand higher wages.

In 1893, Chicago hosted the World's Columbian Exposition, a fair that lasted several months. More than twenty-five million people came to see its exhibits on science, industry, and the arts. George Ferris unveiled the world's first Ferris Wheel at the exposition. It was 250 feet (76 meters) high and could hold 2,160 people.

In 1909, architect Daniel Burnham and his assistant Edward Bennett introduced a landmark plan to keep Chicago beautiful. Their urban plan was the first of its kind in the United States. The Burnham Plan, as it is now called, proposed the creation of more parks and the preservation of the surrounding forest and the natural scenery of the lakefront.

In the first two decades of the twentieth century, the African American population of Chicago exploded. Large numbers looking for employment moved up from the Deep South, more than any other migrant or immigrant group in that period. More than 75,000 African Americans arrived between 1916 and 1918 alone. The unskilled factory jobs they came for were exhausting and underpaid but provided steady work that did not require a formal education.

Reversing Rivers

Reversing the direction of a river is a complicated feat of engineering, but Chicago has done it—twice. Both times the purpose was to reduce the amount of pollution emptying into Lake Michigan. In 1900, the city reversed the flow of the Chicago River. In 1922, they did it again with the Calumet River, which meets Lake Michigan in the city's southeast. As a result of these projects, the pollution ended up in the Mississippi River, almost 300 miles west.

Baseball, the Blues, and Gangsters

In the early twentieth century, Chicago developed a reputation as a vibrant but sometimes wild city. Baseball was becoming the national pastime, and the people of Chicago kicked off a longtime love affair with the sport.

The blues, a musical style with roots in African American songs of hardship, gained popularity in Chicago clubs. In the 1920s,

Chicago musicians helped to launch the Jazz Age, during which musical styles including blues, folk, and ragtime blended to form a new type of dance music: jazz.

The 1920s was also the era of Prohibition, when the United States government banned the manufacture and sale of alcohol. In Chicago, gangsters fought to control the illegal manufacture and sale of liquor. Al Capone ran one of the city's most ruthless and prosperous criminal organizations. Though his name became infamous due to the murders for which he was responsible, Capone was ultimately jailed for tax evasion, the only crime of which he could be convicted .

Louis Armstrong

Just as Chicago is known for jazz music, jazz is known for Louis Armstrong. One of the most influential jazz musicians of the twentieth century, Armstrong spent several early years of his career in Chicago, a hot city for jazz. Musicians could earn good money there, so Armstrong came from New Orleans in 1922. His talent with a cornet earned him a spot with one of the city's most popular bands, the Creole Jazz Band. In 1925, Armstrong began recording under his own name for the first time with small bands of musicians called the Hot Five *and the* Hot Seven. *Their tracks, recorded in Chicago from 1925 to 1928, featured Armstrong's brilliant cornet and trumpet solos and scat singing, and are considered some of the greatest of all jazz recordings.*

The Great Depression settled over the United States in the 1930s, and Chicago was not spared. For decades, workers of different origins had worked alongside each other in factories, but they did not always get along. It took an event as devastating as the Great Depression for them to recognize that the financial crisis affected them all, no matter where they were from. Learning from this new perspective, they were able to cooperate better and organize their unions in a more productive way. Today, Chicago is still a strong union town.

Contributions and Advances

During World War II, Chicago contributed considerably to the war effort. Aircraft factory employment boomed to meet the demand. A large percentage of the influx of workers was African American, and the city passed antidiscrimination laws so they could find jobs and housing. Experiments conducted by scientists at the University of Chicago led to the world's first controlled atomic reactions, a feat that would have a decisive impact on the war when the United States dropped atomic bombs on the Japanese cities of Hiroshima and Nagasaki in 1945.

Since the 1930s, Chicago's city government had been dominated by political machines, or politicians who used dishonest or outright illegal methods such as bribes to maintain control. This era of political manipulation culminated with Richard J. Daley, who was Chicago's mayor

from 1955 until he died in office in 1976. During his six terms, people accused his administration of deep, perpetual corruption. They said that Daley gave jobs to certain people so they would help him get reelected. Some disapproved of the hostile way he reacted to demonstrators who protested the Vietnam War at the 1968 Democratic Convention. The demonstrators and law enforcement clashed brutally.

Despite these incidents, Daley's time as mayor was marked by advancements in Chicago. The city built four expressways, many office buildings, and O'Hare International Airport, named in honor of

▲ *In 1979, Jane Byrne, seen here campaigning downtown, became Chicago's first female mayor. In her inaugural address, promoting multicultural unity, she said, "I pledge tonight to be Mayor for all of the people of this city—for one Chicago."*

heroic World War II naval pilot Lieutenant Commander Edward "Butch" O'Hare, whose plane disappeared during combat in 1943.

Richard M. Daley, Richard J. Daley's son, was elected mayor of Chicago in 1989. He started his fifth term in office in 2004. Under his leadership, Chicago parks are cleaner and the quality of Chicago schools is improving.

CHAPTER 2

People of Chicago

About 70 percent of Illinois's twelve million people reside in the Chicago area. Nearly three million live in the city itself, the majority of them in low-rise, two- to four-story neighborhoods that spread out from the city center. The median age is 31.

The population of the city peaked in 1950 at just over 3,600,000. For the next forty years, population declined as people left for the suburbs. From 1990, however, this trend was reversed, and the population began to rise again, in part because sizable numbers of immigrants moved to the city.

"Chicago will give you a chance. The sporting spirit is the spirit of Chicago."

—Lincoln Steffens, journalist, *The Autobiography of Lincoln Steffens*, 1931.

Modern-day Immigrants

The Chicago metropolitan area is home to 1.4 million immigrants, who make up 17 percent of its population. The post-war period marked the first time more immigrants settled in the suburbs of Chicago than the city itself, since homes were generally more affordable in the suburbs, and more jobs were available there than ever before.

◄ *The Puerto Rico Day Parade in Chicago draws thousands of spectators every June.*

The 1970 census indicated a sizable number of immigrants from Europe, notably Poland, Germany, Italy, Sweden, Ireland, Russia, and Ukraine. The increase in the 1990s was due largely to two groups: Between 1990 and 2000, the number of Asians rose 27 percent and the number of Spanish-speaking people from Latin America increased 38 percent. Currently, Mexicans, Poles, and Asian Indians are the largest immigrant groups in Chicago, together making up more than half of the immigrant population.

Immigrants confront obstacles that native-born Chicagoans do not. Many do not have a college degree and have neither the money nor the language skills to pursue one, preventing them from filling well-paid jobs. Others do not even have a high school degree, which may limit their opportunities even more. In addition, not all Chicago immigrants become United States citizens. Without naturalization status, immigrants cannot vote, which makes it harder to let politicians know what their needs are.

As do many American cities, Chicago attracts illegal immigrants in search of work.

"A lot of real Chicago lives in the neighborhood taverns. It is the mixed German and Irish and Polish gift to the city, a bit of the old country grafted into a strong new plant in the new."

—Bill Granger, writer, 1983.

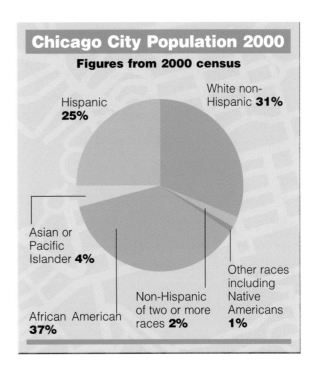

Chicago City Population 2000
Figures from 2000 census

Hispanic **25%**
White non-Hispanic **31%**
Asian or Pacific Islander **4%**
Other races including Native Americans **1%**
African American **37%**
Non-Hispanic of two or more races **2%**

According to one estimate, at least 200,000 illegal immigrants live in the city, many of them from Mexico.

Ethnic Communities

New York City is often viewed as the capital of diversity, but Chicago has diversity to match it. Waves of immigrants throughout Chicago's history have brought their customs and character to the city.

In the past, some Chicago immigrants lived in neighborhoods with others from their country and rarely ventured beyond the borders of their own communities. New generations born in the United States are often taught both English and the language of their family's homeland.

As in other cities, differences between ethnic groups have caused tension in

17

Chicago. Race riots broke out at various times in the nineteenth and twentieth centuries. In 1919, at least thirty-three people died and many more were injured in a conflict between whites and blacks over the right to use a beach.

Irish

The Irish have long been numerous and politically influential in Chicago. In the nineteenth century, Irish people were among the first immigrants to come to Chicago in search of stockyard employment, fleeing the famine and economic misfortune that crippled Ireland at that time. They put down new roots on the South Side and still maintain a community there. Today, however, people of Irish descent can be found throughout the city. As of 2004, eight Irish Americans have become mayor of Chicago.

Hull House

In 1889, Jane Addams founded Hull House on the West Side as a health and education center for the poor of Chicago. Through it, Addams helped hundreds of immigrants who were struggling in their new country. Hull House offered them a library, a nursery school, and one of the first gymnasiums in the country. In 1931, Addams shared the Nobel Peace Prize for her social reform work. The Hull House buildings still standing today are part of the University of Illinois campus.

African Americans

African Americans comprise more than one-third of Chicago's population, their second largest concentration in any U.S. city. In the early twentieth century, many came from southern states and settled on Chicago's South Side to be near both transit lines and the plants where they could find work. After World War II, communities of the African American population expanded to areas of the West and North Sides.

Latinos

Latinos (Spanish-speaking people from Mexico, Central and South America, and the Caribbean) make up about one-quarter of the city's population. Their numbers have grown rapidly since 1960. Mexicans began to migrate in large numbers in the 1940s to work in the railroad and meatpacking industries. Many settled in the Pilsen neighborhood on the Lower West Side and created a community loyal to its Spanish heritage, evident in the festivals, mosaics of Spanish figures, and social activism there. Many Latinos in Chicago participate in fundraisers to help out Latinos in developing countries.

Cities within the City

Some Chicago neighborhoods resemble miniature versions of the inhabitants' home country. For example, Humboldt Park is a predominantly Latino neighborhood whose signs are in Spanish and whose border is marked with a stone arch decorated with

▲ *Mexican Americans wave Mexican flags during Chicago's Mexican Independence Parade.*

the colors of the Puerto Rican flag. Other neighborhoods give little visual indication of the backgrounds of their residents.

The Polish community in Chicago is the largest in the United States. Many of the churches that Polish immigrants built in the 1920s still stand today. The Polish Museum of America, on the North Side, displays paintings, sculptures, and historical artifacts as well as exhibits on the lives of famous Polish Americans.

Swedish, German, and Jewish neighborhoods are located on the Northwest and North sides. Andersonville is a largely Swedish neighborhood adorned with turn-of-the-century homes. Though the Swedish feel of the area has waned as new ethnicities arrive, delis and bakeries there still sell imported Scandinavian treats.

The Ukrainian community on the West Side is home to more than ten thousand people. In this twenty-eight-block village, Ukrainian restaurants and specialty shops line the streets, and the Ukrainian Institute of Modern Art and the Ukrainian National Museum preserve Ukrainian American heritage and culture. One of the main branches of the Ukrainian Greek Catholic Church—the church to which the majority of Ukrainian Americans belong—is in this area. So, too, is Holy Trinity Russian Orthodox Cathedral, designed by the famous architect Louis Sullivan in 1899.

One area of the North Side, centered on Devon Avenue, is home to both a Jewish and

◀ *Most older Indian women in the Indian district of Chicago wear their traditional clothes anytime they are out. Teenagers often wear jeans to school then change into traditional Indian clothes at home.*

Szechuan, and Cantonese cuisine, and shops sell Chinese tea and spices. Chinese architecture decorates the main square.

Little Italy is located just west of the Loop, so close that the skyscrapers loom large. The neighborhood is no longer exclusively Italian. Beginning in the 1960s, African Americans began to compete with Italians for housing in the area, turning it into an unplanned—and mostly harmonious—model of racial integration.

Religious Life

About four out of ten people in both the city and the Chicago metropolitan area are Catholics. This is mainly because many of the city's largest immigrant groups came originally from Catholic countries such as Ireland, Poland, Italy, and Mexico. Other prominent faiths in Chicago include Protestantism, Islam, Judaism, and Buddhism.

The city contains more than one thousand Christian churches. St. Patrick's Church, dedicated in 1856, is Chicago's oldest English-language church. K.A.M. Isaiah Israel Temple, a combination of two synagogues dating back to 1847 and 1852, was the first organized Jewish congregation in the city. Today, it is one of more than fifty synagogues. Chicago's first mosque opened in 1956, and now there are several dozen.

an Asian community that includes Indians and Pakistanis, and a broad range of their businesses—from Muslim grocery stores to beauty shops offering a type of temporary tattoo that uses an Indian ink called henna. Many women there wear traditional dresses called saris, favored by Hindus; others wear a head scarf; some wear the veil. Shop signs are written variously in Hebrew, Arabic, or Sanskrit letters, with English added as well.

Chinatown on the South Side is a crowded, colorful district. Restaurants offer Mandarin,

Festivals

Nearly every weekend, from May to October, at least one Chicago neighborhood hosts an annual festival. In late June and early July, the Taste of Chicago festival fills Grant Park with a variety of cuisines, aromas, and live music. Hundreds of local eateries set up booths and sell a mouth-watering array of food of every imaginable type.

The Chinatown Summer Fair brightens Chicago's streets every July. It includes martial arts demonstrations, races, speeches by dignitaries of Chinese background, and a traditional lion dance, in which people dressed as a large lion parade past the audience to bring good luck.

Despite its name, the Berghoff Oktoberfest, an event at which people sample beer, is held in September. A similar event, the German-American Festival, takes place in an old German neighborhood at Lincoln Square, also in September.

Chicago also holds about two hundred parades a year. The St. Patrick's Day Parade first marched through Chicago in 1843. To celebrate St. Patrick's Day, the Chicago River is dyed dark green, although the brightness of the vegetable dye used lasts only a few hours. Chicagoans are known to say, "On St. Patrick's Day, everyone is Irish."

The Polish Constitution Day Parade, first held in 1891, takes place every May. Many Polish Americans, including war veterans, participate in this televised event. The parade has been especially meaningful to Polish Americans since it marched through Chicago in years when holding such an event in Poland itself was prohibited.

▼ *Worshipers in the Mosque of the Nation of Islam. Around 400,000 Muslims live in the Chicago area.*

CHAPTER 3

Living in Chicago

In Chicago, homes and businesses often coexist on the same street. Sometimes they even coexist within the same building, as is the case with the John Hancock Center downtown. While certain districts may be known for their offices, shops, or homes, many neighborhoods contain a mixture of the three.

"I've been amused, intrigued, outraged, enthralled, and exasperated by Chicago. And I've come to love this American giant, viewing it as the most misunderstood, most underrated city in the world."

—Irv Kupcinet, newspaper columnist and broadcaster nicknamed "Mr. Chicago," 1941.

Architecture

The architecture of Chicago is among the most accomplished in the country—some say the world. From elegant mansions to breathtaking high-rises, Chicago has a broad range of styles.

After the Great Fire of 1871, Chicago had to rebuild itself from virtually nothing. Instead of duplicating what it had been

◀ *People in Chicago have abundant shopping options. Among the city's large malls are The Shops at the Mart and Water Tower Place.*

before, the city builders reinvented Chicago for a modern age. Their most striking innovation was the skyscraper, the first of which were built in the 1880s. Talented architects whose work went up in Chicago before World War I were Louis Sullivan and Dankmar Adler.

One of the United States' most famous architects, Frank Lloyd Wright, lived in Chicago. Wright designed a series of homes whose design became known as Prairie style, including the Robie House, finished in 1909. They were low, long buildings made with natural materials that were meant to blend in with, not disrupt, their

▼ *The entrance facade of the Chicago Place shopping center on Chicago's Magnificent Mile.*

surroundings. Inside, Prairie-style homes had a central chimney, open space, and ample light.

After World War II, Chicago tore down some historic buildings to make way for commercial space. Today, Chicagoans would not let that happen. They are devoted to preserving their past, and many landmarks are now protected by law. As an alternative, the city is gradually revitalizing rundown areas and erecting new buildings there.

Rich and Poor

In parts of Chicago, wealthy neighborhoods and underprivileged neighborhoods are within blocks of one another. The wealthiest sections are mostly white neighborhoods on the North Side, such as

Gold Coast, Lincoln Park, Wrigleyville, Lakeview, and Wicker Park. Many people migrate to the suburbs as their incomes rise, but they often live in neighborhoods that are largely segregated by ethnic origin.

Like many cities, Chicago has sections of extreme poverty. The poorest neighborhoods are on the West and South Sides. They consist predominantly of populations that include African Americans and Latinos. In 2002, 19 percent of the people in Chicago lived below the poverty

"Chicago seems a big city instead of merely a large place."

—A. J. Liebling, journalist, 1949.

level. Of these, 28 percent were under the age of eighteen. Approximately 30 percent of African Americans, 20 percent of Latinos, 18 percent of Asians, and 8.2 percent of whites in Chicago live in poverty.

In the 1990s, poverty among all Chicagoans dropped. African Americans and Latinos made economic gains, but neither group improved their financial situations at the same rate as whites. This economic difference divides the city

▼ *Neighborhoods such as this one, near the area between Rush Street and The Magnificent Mile, are well-preserved reminders of Chicago's earlier years.*

Cabrini-Green

Every city has its poor neighborhoods, but few in America have gained the notoriety of Chicago's Cabrini-Green. In 1942, the first buildings of this public housing development on the North Side were constructed for low-income people of any color. Over the next few decades, the living conditions within the red and white tenements near downtown Chicago worsened, due in part to lack of support from the city government. Cabrini-Green became an area with a mostly black population. The poor stayed poor and did not leave. Unemployment soared. A community that had started with promise deteriorated into a breeding ground for gangs, drugs, and guns. In the 2000s, Chicago began to revitalize Cabrini-Green. The city tore down the high-rises to make way for new luxury buildings. In some of them, it is planned that people of varied incomes will live side by side. Some displaced Cabrini-Green families have been allowed to apply for apartments in the new development, which will be paid for by the city.

socially, sometimes hindering city government efforts to desegregate. Chicago officials know there are many problems to address, such as drug use and dilapidated tenement buildings. In the past, the city government has built low-rent housing for people in need. Though such housing has been a positive step, it does not decrease crime or slum conditions in every case. Private institutions have also funded the development of housing in some communities. This new housing, combined with social programs and services to help the residents get jobs, has met with some success.

Fierce Weather

At times, nature wreaks havoc in Chicago. In 1967 and 1979, severe blizzards dumped record-setting amounts of snow on the city. Chicago sent plowed snow to Florida by train as a gift for children who had never seen it. In 1915, 1916, 1955, and 1995, Chicagoans experienced oppressive heat waves. In July of each of those years, the temperature spiked higher than normal, sometimes over 100°F (38°C). More than five hundred people died from the heat in 1995, many of them elderly. Even tornadoes have ripped through the Chicago area, in 1961 and 1967.

Homelessness

Estimates vary, but on any given night, the Chicago area has at least 15,000 homeless people. Each year, between 80,000 to 166,000 people are without a home at some point. Many of them remain on the streets for months or longer. Long-term homeless people often suffer from severe health problems, which are made worse by Chicago's bitter winter weather.

More than three-quarters of the homeless people in Chicago are African American, and almost 40 percent are families. Young homeless people often miss school or drop out altogether. Officials in Chicago city government and human rights activists recognize the seriousness of the situation and are working on ways to place the homeless in permanent housing rather than shelters.

Crime

Hollywood has romanticized Chicago's historic connection to crime in movies about gangsters. In reality, crime was not glamorous then, nor is it today. The gangsters of the 1920s have given way to the street gangs of the present, who still fight to control territory in which they can sell drugs.

Even though its homicide rate in 2003 was the lowest in ten years, Chicago had more murders than any other large American city, and gang conflict was the largest cause. Almost every other category of criminal activity showed a decrease from the previous year.

In the twenty-first century, Chicago is one of several cities in the country to begin installing a controversial system of surveillance cameras in high-crime neighborhoods. Police officers can access the cameras from computers and use them to monitor suspicious and outright criminal activity. Some residents feel the cameras are an invasion of privacy, while others feel safer knowing their streets are being watched and hope the cameras will discourage illegal behavior.

Getting Around

Chicagoans use many forms of transportation. For commuters with cars, many roads and expressways feed into the city, but they are very congested. In

▼ *The streets of Chicago are arranged in a grid to make them easy to navigate. The numbering system starts from State Street, which is shown here and runs north and south, and Madison Street, which runs east and west.*

addition, finding a parking space can be frustrating, and garage parking can be costly. Many people prefer cabs to cars because they avoid parking problems. Train and bus services run regularly between the city and the suburbs, and are much cheaper than cabs or cars, so many commuters prefer to use public transportation.

Every day, about half a million people ride the Rapid Transit System, Chicago's train line. In the downtown area it is called the "El" because many of the tracks are elevated, though some are at ground level or underground. Chicago's train system is the city's least expensive, fastest, and most convenient mode of transportation. The system's seven lines reach most neighborhoods and the airports, twenty-four hours a day. Buses are another inexpensive option, but service is often slower than the trains.

Chicago Cuisine

Chicago has a hearty appetite. Restaurants serve international dishes as well as local specialties. More common tastes such as Mexican or Chinese are plentiful, but Chicago also offers exotic fare including Ethiopian and Pakistani. Barbecue rib joints are a leftover of the city's history with the meatpacking industry. Deep dish pizza, developed in Chicago in 1953, is still popular. Another treat that was introduced in Chicago is Cracker Jack,® a caramel-covered mix of popcorn and peanuts.

Chicago is a hub for Amtrak, the national train service. In 2003, Chicago's Amtrak station was one of the country's top five busiest. Chicago's two main airports are O'Hare International, 17 miles (27 kilometers) northwest of downtown, and Midway, 12 miles (19 km) southwest of downtown. O'Hare, the larger of the two, is the world's busiest airport.

Education

More than 400,000 young people attend school in Chicago. The Board of Education oversees the Chicago Public Schools district, which includes over six hundred schools. Compared to other regions' school achievement levels, Chicago's schools have ranked low in recent years.

To strengthen the Chicago school system, public school officials are focusing on both the students and the facilities. They are determined to raise literacy by hiring better-trained teachers. Officials are also working to bring more technology into classrooms and to provide more extracurricular programs after school and during the summer.

School overcrowding is another serious issue that the Chicago public school system is addressing. About 30 percent of Chicago students attend overcrowded schools. A large portion of the budget goes to building new facilities.

In addition, many existing school buildings need repair. Some have leaky roofs, broken windows, flaking lead paint, and other hazards. Since 2002, the public

▲ *A teacher helps young children with their reading.*
Tackling low literacy is one of the Chicago school
system's priorities.

school system has spent more than $2.4 billion to improve their schools, but they need almost double that amount to complete all needed renovations.

The Roman Catholic parochial schools in Chicago make up the nation's largest private school system, educating at least 100,000 students in more than three hundred schools. Chicago also has private schools affiliated with other religions and some with no religious affiliation.

Many colleges and universities are located in or around Chicago. Currently, the public university with the highest attendance is the University of Illinois at Chicago, with more than 24,000 students. DePaul University (more than 19,000 students) and Northwestern University (more than 17,000) are the private universities with the highest attendance. The University of Chicago—with 12,000 students—has the best reputation of all Chicago's universities.

As well as providing a wide range of universities, Chicago also offers students a number of specialty schools. The Art Institute of Chicago is a world-class museum that has a fine arts college connected to it. Other schools teach music, business, and law.

CHAPTER 4

Chicago at Work

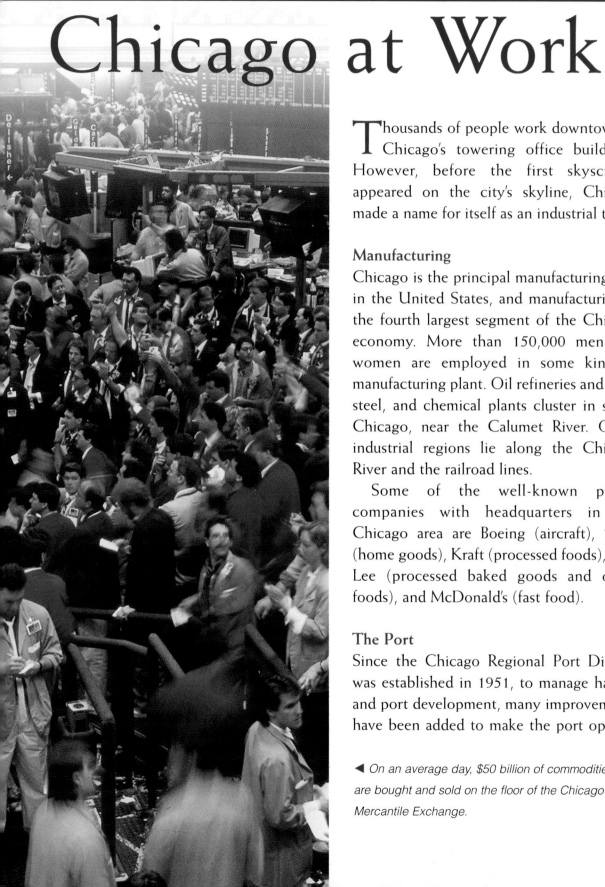

Thousands of people work downtown in Chicago's towering office buildings. However, before the first skyscraper appeared on the city's skyline, Chicago made a name for itself as an industrial town.

Manufacturing

Chicago is the principal manufacturing city in the United States, and manufacturing is the fourth largest segment of the Chicago economy. More than 150,000 men and women are employed in some kind of manufacturing plant. Oil refineries and iron, steel, and chemical plants cluster in south Chicago, near the Calumet River. Other industrial regions lie along the Chicago River and the railroad lines.

Some of the well-known public companies with headquarters in the Chicago area are Boeing (aircraft), Sears (home goods), Kraft (processed foods), Sara Lee (processed baked goods and other foods), and McDonald's (fast food).

The Port

Since the Chicago Regional Port District was established in 1951, to manage harbor and port development, many improvements have been added to make the port operate

◄ *On an average day, $50 billion of commodities are bought and sold on the floor of the Chicago Mercantile Exchange.*

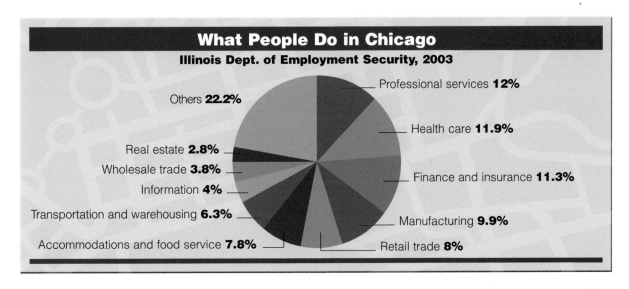

What People Do in Chicago
Illinois Dept. of Employment Security, 2003

- Others **22.2%**
- Professional services **12%**
- Health care **11.9%**
- Real estate **2.8%**
- Wholesale trade **3.8%**
- Information **4%**
- Finance and insurance **11.3%**
- Transportation and warehousing **6.3%**
- Manufacturing **9.9%**
- Accommodations and food service **7.8%**
- Retail trade **8%**

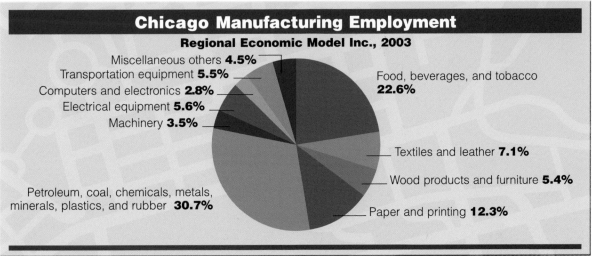

Chicago Manufacturing Employment
Regional Economic Model Inc., 2003

- Miscellaneous others **4.5%**
- Transportation equipment **5.5%**
- Computers and electronics **2.8%**
- Electrical equipment **5.6%**
- Machinery **3.5%**
- Food, beverages, and tobacco **22.6%**
- Textiles and leather **7.1%**
- Wood products and furniture **5.4%**
- Petroleum, coal, chemicals, metals, minerals, plastics, and rubber **30.7%**
- Paper and printing **12.3%**

▲ *These charts show the variety of occupations of men and women in Chicago. Almost one out of every ten workers is employed in manufacturing industries.*

more efficiently, such as the installation of grain elevators to move heavy loads. Companies from around the world ship freight through the port of Chicago, but it is especially desirable for Midwest companies, since shipping on water can be less expensive than shipping over land. More than seven hundred miles inland from the Atlantic, the port also offers warehousing and consultation on shipping fragile and perishable cargoes.

Finance

The Chicago Stock Exchange, located downtown, is the third most active stock exchange in the country. A stock exchange the largest commodity market in the United States, where products are traded, bought, and sold. Many of the commodities traded in Chicago are agricultural or industrial. Commodities, precious metals, and currencies are also traded at the Chicago Mercantile Exchange. Chicago is home to several major insurance companies as well.

Printing and Publishing

Some of the largest printing plants in the United States are located in the Chicago area, producing mail-order catalogs and telephone directories as well as a variety of newspapers, books, and magazines. Some Chicago publishers specialize in encyclopedias and educational material.

▲ At this plant of the Ford Motor Company, the human element is still essential in building cars.

is a hall in which people buy and sell stocks (small parts of ownership of companies). The floor, or main area, of the Chicago Stock Exchange is an energetic place— people shout as they do business and move fast all day. The Chicago Board of Trade is

Harpo Studios

The Oprah Winfrey Show, *a daily talk show in which host Oprah Winfrey encourages viewers and helps people find happiness, debuted in Chicago in 1986. Because of Winfrey's intelligence, positive message, and upbeat personality, the program has been at the top of the ratings ever since. Winfrey is now one of the nation's most successful entertainers and public figures. The show is filmed at Winfrey's Harpo ("Oprah" spelled backwards) Studios in Chicago. Winfrey bought a former armory in 1988 and transformed it into a state-of-the-art production facility. Over 21 million people in America, and many more throughout the world, watch her award-winning program every week.*

Others produce trade publications, or magazines targeted to a specific industry. These are usually available only by subscription, not in stores. In terms of editorial activity in the United States, the city is second only to New York.

The daily newspapers with the largest circulation are the *Chicago Tribune*, which hit the stands in 1847, and the *Chicago Sun-Times*, which has been published since 1929. The *Chicago Daily Defender* is aimed at the city's African American citizens. Other smaller newspapers are published

"My first day in Chicago—September 4, 1983. I set foot in this city, and just walking down the street, it was like roots, like the motherland. I knew I belonged here."

—Oprah Winfrey, national talk-show host and producer, whose daily show originates in Chicago.

▼ *When he was running for president, Al Gore appeared on* The Oprah Winfrey Show *in Chicago. The show is broadcast throughout the United States.*

Sears Tower

When the Sears Tower opened in 1973, it was the tallest building in the world, at a height of 1,450 feet (442 meters). After the Petronas Twin Towers in Malaysia were completed in 1996, the Sears Tower slipped to number two. However, it remains the tallest building in the United States, with 110 floors and more than one hundred elevators. By elevator, it takes about one minute to reach the observation deck on the 103rd floor, which is open to the public. On a clear day, four states—Illinois, Michigan, Wisconsin, and Indiana—are visible from it. Sears moved its headquarters to a suburb in the early 1990s, and now other companies occupy the Sears Tower.

throughout the metropolitan area on a daily, weekly, or monthly basis. Some are geared toward specific ethnic communities and may be in non-English languages.

Conventions and Trade Shows

On an average day, thousands of people who do not live anywhere near Chicago are doing business there. The city hosts more conventions and trade shows a year than any other in the United States. Conventions are held in immense halls in which exhibitors have booths to display their products or services. Since so many people visit these shows, Chicago has a large number of hotels to accommodate them.

Unemployment

Currently, between 6 and 7 percent of Chicagoans who want to work are unemployed. About half of them want blue-collar jobs while the other half seek white-collar jobs. A 2001 study found that approximately 100,000 people in Chicago between the ages of sixteen and twenty-four were jobless and not in school.

City Government

The city government of Chicago consists of two branches, executive and legislative. The mayor is the chief executive and the city council is the legislative body.

The fifty members of the city council each represent one of the city's fifty wards, or districts. They are elected by the citizens of the wards and usually meet on a monthly basis to discuss and pass ordinances, or laws of the city. They also approve certain budgetary matters of the city, such as land acquisition and traffic control.

The mayor is the city's top public official, elected by the citizens over age 18 for a four-year term. One person can serve as mayor as many times as he or she is elected. The mayor oversees the city council, and together they appoint the heads of departments, such as the Board of Education, Park District, and Housing Authority. If a city council vote results in a tie, the mayor casts the deciding vote.

Besides the mayor, two other city government positions are elected, the clerk and the treasurer. The clerk is in charge of all official city documents and keeps the city council records. The treasurer is responsible for the financial records of the city.

Services Provided

Running a city that has more than 100 hospitals, 3,700 miles (5,950 km) of streets, 13,000 police officers, and 30,000,000 annual visitors is no easy task. The City of Chicago employs about forty thousand people in more than forty departments. Among them are firefighters, police officers, sanitation workers, agents in the Department of Animal Care and Control, and the staff of the Chicago Public Library. The city pays their salaries by taxing the citizens who benefit from their services. Income, property, and goods purchased are all taxed for that purpose.

Famous Mayors

Chicago has had several famous mayors. Two pairs of fathers and sons have been mayor. The first pair was Carter Harrison, Sr., and Carter Harrison, Jr. Each was elected five times. Harrison, Sr., was first elected in 1879 and Harrison, Jr., was first elected in 1897. The other father-son mayoral pair was Richard J. Daley and Richard M. Daley. Richard J. Daley was elected six times, first in 1955. His son, the current mayor, has been elected five times, first in 1989. Jane Byrne was the first female mayor of Chicago. She served from 1979 to 1983. Harold Washington, the first African American mayor, was elected twice, first in 1983.

▼ *Firefighters tackle a blaze in one of the older buildings in Chicago.*

CHAPTER 5

Chicago at Play

Whether people would rather move their bodies or be moved by art, "shop 'til they drop," or shimmy to sweet sounds, Chicago can keep them entertained. Many of Chicago's attractions have a superlative attached—the largest this, the best that—but people often agree that the superlatives are well deserved. Tourists can see the sites by open-topped double-decker bus, horse-drawn carriage, or take a harbor boat tour during the summer months.

Art and Science

Chicago has nearly fifty museums, many of them top-rated. Though some are clustered in the center of the city, there are welcoming museums in many other neighborhoods, too, some offering free admission.

The Art Institute of Chicago, founded in 1866, is one of the world's most prestigious art museums. Located in Grant Park by Lake Michigan, the Art Institute showcases art from five thousand years ago up to the present and from all around the world. Painting, especially French Impressionist and post-Impressionist painting, and sculpture feature strongly, but there are also

◀ *Few athletes in the late twentieth century inspired as loyal a fan base as gifted Chicago Bulls basketball star Michael Jordan.*

Navy Pier

Navy Pier is Chicago's most popular tourist destination. About eight million people a year flock to this entertainment complex located east of downtown. It includes shops, restaurants, the Chicago Children's Museum, and a fifteen-story Ferris Wheel. Once a rotting wharf on Lake Michigan, it was renovated and opened in 1995. Sightseeing boat cruises depart from Navy Pier daily.

photographs, furniture, ceramics, textiles, and decorative artifacts in this huge and diverse collection.

The Museum of Contemporary Art on East Chicago Avenue is the world's largest modern art museum. Founded in 1967, it displays work by international and local artists, including film, video, and multimedia presentations.

On East Washington Street, several blocks from the Art Institute of Chicago, is the Chicago Cultural Center. It features art galleries and free concerts, films, and lectures. The Cultural Center also contains the Museum of Broadcast Communications, which plays and screens programs from the early days of radio and television.

The Museum of Science and Industry on the South Side close to Lake Michigan is housed within the only surviving structure from the 1893 World's Columbian Exposition. Many of its exhibits are computerized and interactive, including models of a brain and heart, a coal mine, a real World War II German submarine (captured in battle), and a space shuttle.

In Grant Park, the Field Museum of Natural History and the Adler Planetarium are big draws for those interested in archeology, nature, and astronomy. In 1997, the Field Museum obtained the most complete and best preserved fossil skeleton of a Tyrannosaurus rex ever found. Among its other attractions are an interactive exhibit that simulates life underground and a full-size reconstruction of an Egyptian tomb. The Adler Planetarium, which opened in 1930, holds a variety of daily sky shows and also offers a virtual-reality ride through the universe.

Other specialized museums include the Du Sable Museum of African American History in Washington Park and the Chicago Children's Museum on Navy Pier.

Wild Kingdoms

Opened in 1930, the John G. Shedd Aquarium in Grant Park displays sea creatures great and small. Many aquatic habitats have been recreated there, including a Caribbean reef, the Amazon Basin, and the North American Pacific Coast. The attached Oceanarium, overlooking Lake Michigan, houses large marine mammals such as beluga whales, dolphins, and three species of penguins.

Founded in 1868, the Lincoln Park Zoo is alongside Lake Michigan on the North Side. Entry is free, and, among many attractions, visitors can study the behavior of a menagerie of fruit bats, enormous monitor lizards, gorilla families, and several species of rain forest monkeys. With luck, visitors will also see the chimpanzees drawing on poster board with crayons.

Sports Mania

Few cities have sports fans as passionate as Chicago's. They stand by their teams when they lose and cheer loudly when they win. Some men are so dedicated that they take off their shirts at football games to reveal supportive slogans painted on their chests—even in winter.

Chicago has two major league baseball teams, the White Sox and the Cubs. The White Sox, who play at US Cellular Field (formerly Comiskey Park) on the South Side, last won the World Series in 1917. Based in Wrigley Field on the North Side, the Cubs last won the World Series in 1908. Although both teams have not had any major successes for a very long time, their loyal fans continue to support them.

Chicago's National Football League (NFL) team is the Bears. They play at Soldier Field in Grant Park. The Bears won the Super Bowl in 1986. On the West Side is the United Center, where Chicago's professional basketball team, the Bulls, and its NHL hockey team, the Blackhawks, play.

People who like to participate in sports have a multitude of options in Chicago. The

▲ *The Chicago Cubs baseball team plays at Wrigley Field, an old-fashioned ballpark where the score is still changed by hand.*

city has nearly eight hundred baseball and softball diamonds and more than six hundred tennis courts. It also has basketball courts, gymnasiums, swimming pools, and golf courses.

Shores and Parks

When Americans think about Midwest cities, beaches are probably not the first feature that comes to mind. Chicago, however, boasts thirty miles of lakefront, fifteen miles of which are soft, sandy beaches. An 18-mile (29-km) paved lakeside path is used by cyclists, walkers, and in-line skaters.

Lake Michigan beckons to water sports enthusiasts of many kinds. Private boats, from yachts to kayaks, bob on the surface. Water-skiers and jet-skiers skim across the lake all summer, and parasailers soar above. In some places, people can swim in the lake.

Other bodies of water throughout the city are also available for leisure activities. People paddleboat in the pond in Lincoln Park, and many park lagoons are stocked for fishing.

The city has a vast park system, both near the water and inland. Grant Park is

39

From Athletics to Celebrities

Some of Chicago's professional athletes have taken on legendary status. Michael Jordan led the Bulls to six National Basketball Association (NBA) championships in the 1990s. He also appeared in movies and even played professional baseball for a short time. In 1998, Sammy Sosa, who played for the Cubs, raced Mark McGwire, who played for the St. Louis Cardinals, to break a longstanding single season home-run record. They both succeeded, and the news made national headlines.

centrally located near the lakeside. Sculptures and monuments dot its grassy, 200-acre (81-hectare) landscape, as does Buckingham Fountain, the world's largest illuminated fountain. Family-friendly Lincoln Park is Chicago's largest green space.

In winter after heavy snowfall, the parks and forest preserves in and around Chicago provide cross-country skiing, snowmobiling areas, and toboggan runs.

Sing the Blues and More

Chicago is a city with a soundtrack of soulful music. The city is crammed with nightclubs and lounges where musicians jam late into the night. Many people find the blues uplifting, despite the name. Blues greats, including Muddy Waters and Bo Diddley, recorded music in Chicago. Music buffs attend the Chicago Blues Festival and Chicago Jazz Festival each summer. Rock and country are also part of the sound of Chicago, and many local bands have gone on to national prominence.

▼ *Located in Grant Park beside Lake Michigan, Buckingham Fountain offers light and water spectacles daily from dusk to 11:00 p.m.*

"*Anywhere in the world you hear a Chicago bluesman play, it's a Chicago sound born and bred.*"

—Ralph Metcalfe, congressman.

The Chicago Symphony Orchestra has an international reputation. The musical ensemble regularly plays for sold-out audiences at the new Symphony Hall, and is known for performing contemporary as well as classical pieces. The 186-member Symphony Chorus sometimes sings with the orchestra. Most performances at the Lyric Opera of Chicago are also sold out.

▲ *Jazz music can be considered the soundtrack of the city, tracing its roots in Chicago back to the early decades of the twentieth century.*

Chicago has a dynamic theater scene. The city's actors put on mainstream Broadway musicals and comedies, as well as experimental plays and intimate dinner theater, many of which earn critical acclaim. Second City, a nationally recognized improvisational comedy troupe, has nurtured many talented performers who have gone on to successful television and film careers. The national TV program *Saturday Night Live* often hires new cast members out of Second City.

CHAPTER 6

Looking Forward

Chicago has a history of setting goals and acting on them. The Burnham Plan of 1909 has been especially inspirational. Burnham is credited with saying, "Make no little plans." His plan encouraged the city to conserve its natural beauty as it grew into a modern city. The people of Chicago listened and did just that. As is often the case, however, with growth come new problems.

A key problem Chicago is encountering today is urban sprawl. Many businesses and residents are leaving the city for less expensive rent or land in the outlying areas. This movement often has a negative effect on a city's economy and environment. When fewer people are in the city, the city makes less money. When more people must commute to work, traffic and pollution get worse.

In 1999, a group of concerned businesspeople called the Commercial Club of Chicago proposed a plan—"Chicago Metropolis 2020"—to fix these problems. In fact, this is the same organization that sponsored the Burnham Plan nearly a century ago. The Burnham Plan was primarily about the appearance of the city, but Chicago Metropolis 2020 addresses the city's economic and social issues.

◄ *Children explore an interactive exhibit about the human brain at Chicago's Museum of Science and Industry. Providing a good education for all young Chicagoans is a priority of the city government.*

One of its suggestions is to expand public transportation to ease road congestion. Another is to build affordable housing nearer to where jobs are. A third is to guarantee every school a minimum amount of financial support so that every child has a better chance of getting a good education. One member of the organization created a booklet to explain the Chicago Metropolis 2020 plan to children, then distributed 100,000 copies to schools.

Chicago is proud of its achievements. It has rebuilt after catastrophe. It has created architecture that is appreciated by people around the world. It has maintained green park space throughout its urban areas and

▼ *Mayor Daley has initiated a program for new runways and remodeling to ease congestion at the world's busiest airport, Chicago's O'Hare International.*

"I Will"

Chicago has a motto that is at once simple and powerful: "I Will." Upon reading about Chicago's history, perhaps voices from the past whisper to you: a nineteenth-century Irish immigrant saying, "I will speak up until my boss improves the working conditions at this factory;" a storeowner after the Great Fire saying, "I will start my business again right away;" or an architect saying, "I will create a building unlike any in this area." This motto reflects the spirit of a tough city.

plans to add more features such as bike and walking paths. Chicago has been described as the "downtown of the Midwest." At the same time, it is a global city. Thanks in part to its bustling O'Hare International Airport, the world stops in Chicago every day.

Almost one hundred years later, Chicago is still listening to Burnham. The city grew tremendously in the twentieth century, literally reaching the sky with its tall towers. Now, in the twenty-first century, Chicago shows few signs of slowing down.

"Chicago is a city of contradictions, of private visions haphazardly overlaid and linked together. If the city was unhappy with itself yesterday—and invariably it was—it will reinvent itself today."

—Pat Colander, writer and editor, 1985.

43

Time Line

ca 8000 B.C. Humans live along the lakeshore in the Chicago area.

A.D. 1673 French-Canadians Louis Jolliet and Jacques Marquette explore the region.

1779 French-Haitian Jean Baptiste Point du Sable establishes the first permanent non-Native settlement in the Chicago region.

1795 Native Americans grant the Chicago region to the United States.

1803 The United States government builds Fort Dearborn in the Chicago region.

1812 Potawatomi Native Americans burn down Fort Dearborn.

1816 Fort Dearborn is rebuilt.

1825 The Erie Canal opens.

1830 Chicago is mapped out.

1833 Chicago is incorporated as a town.

1837 Chicago is incorporated as a city with a population of 4,200.

1848 Illinois and Michigan Canal opens.

1865 The Union Stock Yards open.

1871 The Great Fire kills over three hundred people.

1885 The world's first steel-framed skyscraper is built in Chicago.

1886 Police officers and industrial workers are killed in the Haymarket Riot.

1889 Jane Addams opens Hull House to help immigrants.

1893 Chicago hosts the World's Columbian Exposition, a world fair.

1894 Workers strike against the Pullman railroad car company.

1900 The Chicago River's flow is reversed.

1909 The Burnham Plan to preserve Chicago's beauty is presented.

1922 The Calumet River's flow is reversed.

1931 Gangster Al Capone is jailed.

1955 O'Hare International Airport opens. Richard J. Daley is elected mayor.

1968 Anti-Vietnam War demonstrators and law enforcement clash brutally at the national Democratic Convention.

1973 The Sears Tower opens.

1979 Jane Byrne becomes Chicago's first female mayor.

1983 Harold Washington becomes Chicago's first African American mayor.

1989 Richard M. Daley is elected mayor.

1999 Chicago Metropolis 2020 plan is proposed.

2003 The O'Hare Modernization Act authorizes expansion and remodeling of O'Hare International Airport.

Glossary

affiliation association, connection.

assimilate to become similar to another culture by taking on some of its features.

blue-collar describes people with manual or factory jobs that may require protective clothing.

census a system that counts and categorizes a population.

coalition a temporary alliance of political parties or states.

commuter a person who travels to work, often from a suburb to the city.

consumption the act of consuming or eating; also describes the infectious disease of tuberculosis.

descent a person's derivation from his or her ancestors.

ethnic of a particular nationality, race, or cultural group.

immigration the process of moving from one country to another to live.

integration the act of combining more than one racial or group into a community.

Latino a person of Latin-American descent.

legislature a group that makes, changes, or cancels laws.

literacy the ability to read and write.

meatpacking the business of slaughtering animals and packaging the meat for food.

missionary a person who travels to another country to convert its people to a religion.

National Historic Site an area in the United States protected for its historic significance.

political machine a group of politicians that organizes and uses questionable or dishonest methods to maintain control of a city government.

Prohibition the period from 1920 to 1933 when the United States did not allow alcohol to be made or sold.

slaughterhouse a building where animals are killed so their meat can be prepared as food.

stockyard an enclosed area where cattle or other livestock are kept.

strike a group's refusal to work to protest low pay or inadequate working conditions.

tax evasion the act of not paying the correct amount of tax.

union an organization of employees that is formed to discuss their rights and pay with their employer.

urban sprawl the spreading of developments, such as businesses or shops, outward from a city.

ward an electoral district in a city.

white-collar describes people with salaried jobs that do not require protective clothing.

Further Information

Books

Brent, Lynnette R., and Leslie Morrison. *Chicago.* Heinemann Library, 2002.

Brexel, Bernardette. *The Knights of Labor and the Haymarket Riot: The Fight for an Eight-Hour Workday (America's Industrial Society in the Nineteenth Century).* Rosen Publishing Group, 2004.

Marx, Christy. *The Great Chicago Fire of 1871 (Tragic Fires Throughout History).* Rosen Publishing Group, 2004.

Miller, Robert H. *The Story of Jean Baptiste Du Sable (Stories from the Forgotten West).* Silver Press, 1995.

Murphy, Jim. *The Great Fire.* Scholastic, 1995.

Stein, R. Conrad. *Chicago (Cities of the World).* Children's Press, 1997.

Web Sites

www.cityofchicago.org
Gain facts and information through this official Chicago web site.

www.chipublib.org
Browse through the offerings of the Chicago Public Library.

www.chicagotribune.com
Access the city's largest-circulation daily newspaper.

www.chichildrensmuseum.org
Discover the Chicago Children's Museum.

www.chicagohs.org
Delve more deeply into Chicago's history in the official web site of the Chicago Historical Society.

www.chicago.il.org
See what activities and accommodations are available with the Chicago Convention and Tourism Bureau.

www.sheddaquarium.org
Dive in to the Shedd Aquarium web site.

www.adlerplanetarium.org
Discover the offerings of the Adler Planetarium.

www.navypier.com
Plan your day at Navy Pier.

www.artic.edu
Take a virtual tour of the Art Institute of Chicago.

www.fieldmuseum.org
Explore the variety of exhibits at the Field Museum of Natural History.

Index